DISCOVER AND DO!

ANGLO-SAXONS

GET HANDS-ON WITH HISTORY

Written by Jane Lacey

W

FRANKLIN WATTS

LONDON • SYDNEY

Franklin Watts
First published in Great Britain in 2021
by The Watts Publishing Group
Copyright © The Watts Publishing Group, 2021

Produced for Franklin Watts by
White-Thomson Publishing Ltd
www.wtpub.co.uk

Editor: Katie Dicker
Designer: Clare Nicholas
Series designer: Rocket Design (East Anglia) Ltd

Picture credits:
t=top b=bottom m=middle l=left r=right

Julian Baker *cover/title page l, cover/title page r,* 11t, 29t; iStock:
bortonia 5tl, 16t and 31b, benedek 7t, TonyBaggett 7b and
21m, duncan1890 8t, 12bm, 20bl and 28, Colin13362 12t,
14b and 32, ZU_09 16br and 30t, stevegeer 21t; Shutterstock:
Robert Adrian Hillman 4, 6t and 20br, delcarmat 5tr, 22m
and 30b, Krugalin 5br, 26 and 31t, Oceloti 6–7, perori 8–9b,
3DMI 9t, Janna Golovacheva 10t, Rustic 12–13, NEILRAS 16b,
rudall30 16bl and 29b, MAVRITSINA IRINA 19t, leedsn 19b,
antonpix 22t, Bur_malin 22–23, Jeanie333 23t, jorisvo 24t
and 31m, givi585 24bm, Anastasia Boiko 24–25; Alamy: Jeff
Morgan 05 8bm, World History Archive 14t, Universal Images
Group North America LLC 18b, travelib history 25t, The Print
Collector 26b; Stefan Chabluk 6b; Getty: Dorling Kindersley
10b; Ian Thompson 20t.

All design elements from Shutterstock.
Craft models from a previous series made
by Anna-Marie D'Cruz/photos by Steve Shott.

Every attempt has been made to clear copyright.
Should there be any inadvertent omission, please
apply to the publisher for rectification.

Printed in China

Franklin Watts
An imprint of
Hachette Children's Group
Part of The Watts Publishing Group
Carmelite House
50 Victoria Embankment
London EC4Y 0DZ

An Hachette UK Company
www.hachettechildrens.co.uk

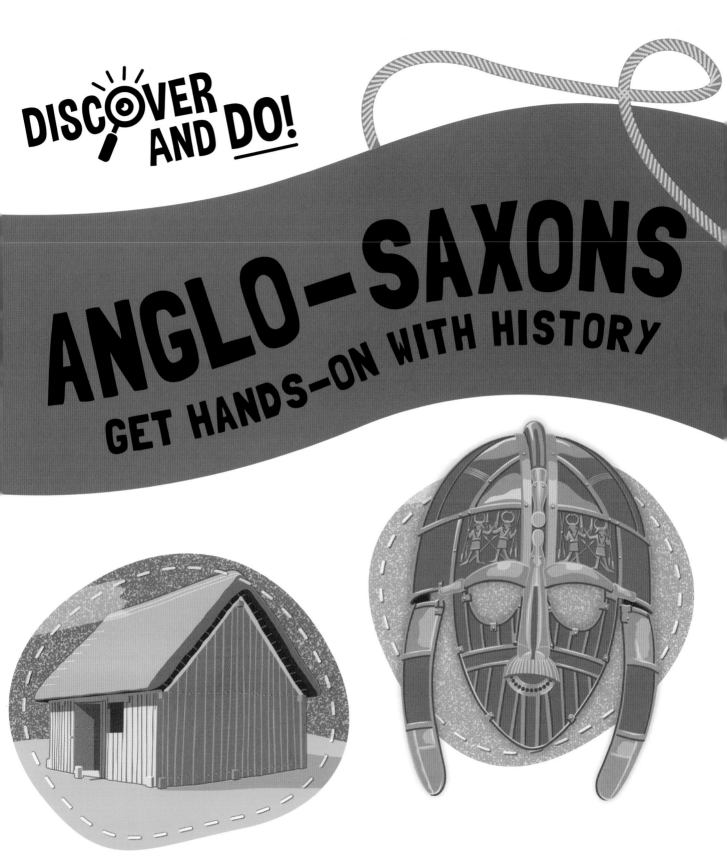

DISCOVER AND DO!

ANGLO-SAXONS

GET HANDS-ON WITH HISTORY

W
FRANKLIN WATTS
LONDON • SYDNEY

CONTENTS

Words that appear in **bold** can be found in the glossary on pages 28–29.

INVASION

The Angles, Saxons and Jutes were **tribes** who lived in northern Europe – what is now northern Germany, Denmark and northern Holland. They **invaded** Britain in the 5th and 6th centuries looking for better farmland where they could settle with their families.

Settlement

The invading tribes landed on the east and south coasts of Britain. They settled and gradually moved further and further inland. The settlers were known as the Anglo-Saxons and their language has become the English we speak today.

The Anglo-Saxons invaded Britain because it had more favourable land and weather conditions.

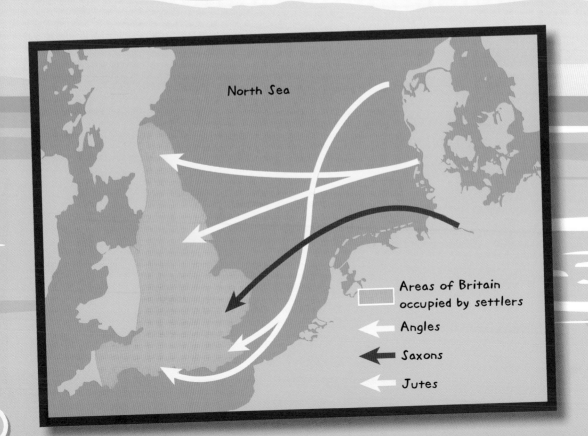

North Sea

Areas of Britain occupied by settlers

Angles

Saxons

Jutes

How do we know?

The Anglo-Saxon Chronicle is a history of Britain written in Anglo-Saxon times. It gives us a year-by-year record of the lives of kings and bishops, of battles and other important events. Discoveries, such as hoards of treasure and the ship burial at Sutton Hoo (see page 18) also tell us important things about the Anglo-Saxons.

This copy of the Anglo-Saxon Chronicle is found in the British Library in London.

A statue of King Alfred the Great (849-899 CE) who ordered the Anglo-Saxon Chronicle to be written and kept up-to-date.

WARRIORS

Anglo-Saxon **warriors** sailed across the North Sea in wooden ships. They fought with huge axes, spears, long swords and long knives. Shields and metal helmets protected their bodies and heads.

Helmets and shields

Wealthy warriors, such as a king or lord, had helmets and shields that were highly decorated. The weapons found at Sutton Hoo are thought to have belonged to a wealthy warrior.

This Anglo-Saxon warrior would have come from a wealthy family.

Anglo-Saxon boats called longships were used to carry soldiers.

Strong defence

Most warrior shields were round. They were made from lime wood, which was light to carry, and some were covered in leather. They had a metal boss in the centre.

MAKE A SHIELD

You will need:
- cardboard box
- metallic card
- scissors
- sticky tape and glue
- pencil and paints

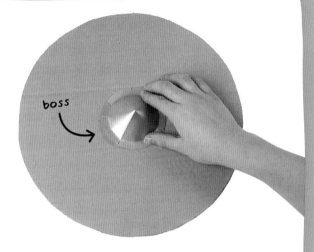

boss

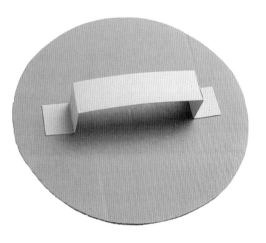

2 To make the boss, cut a circle of metallic card (10 cm diameter). Cut a line from the edge to the centre and bend into a low cone. Snip at 2 cm intervals around the edge to make it easy to stick to the centre of the shield.

3 Paint a simple pattern onto your shield and a circle of brown around the outside.

1 Cut a circle (30 cm diameter) from a cardboard box and then cut a strip of card about 30 cm long. Bend the strip to make a handle and tape across the centre of the circle.

SETTLERS

The Anglo-Saxon invaders built **settlements** and farmed the land. The settlements had a large hall in the centre surrounded by houses and workshops. Animals were kept in pens.

LEIGH, LEY
wood clearing

WICK
farm

FELD
field

FORD
river crossing

TON
village

Look out for local places that have Anglo-Saxon words in their name.

Place names

'Ham' was the Anglo-Saxon word for settlement, 'den' was a hill and 'worth' meant enclosed by a hedge. So the towns of Swaffham, Eversden and Boxworth in East Anglia, UK, were once Anglo-Saxon settlements.

You can see the hall at the centre of this Anglo-Saxon village.

Living quarters

Anglo-Saxon houses has one big room where the family cooked, ate and slept. They had one door and a window that usually faced south to catch the sunlight.

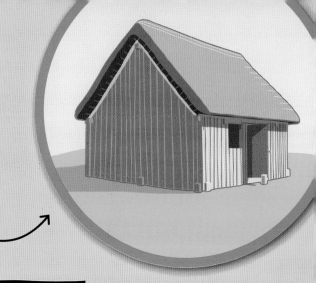

Anglo-Saxon houses were made from wood with a **thatched** roof.

MAKE AN ANGLO-SAXON VILLAGE

You will need:
- **small card boxes**
- **sheets of card**
- **pencil and ruler**
- **scissors**
- **brown and yellow paint**
- **black felt-tip pen**
- **raffia**
- **sticky tape or glue**

1 Use small boxes to make the base of each building. Draw a door 4 cm wide and 3 cm high on one side. Cut along one side and along the top and fold back the door.

2 Fold rectangles of card in half lengthways for the roofs – the rectangle should be as long as each box.

3 Paint the walls brown and add lines to look like wooden planks. Paint the roof to look like thatch (or stick on strips of raffia). Make a base from a piece of card and use raffia to make animal pens.

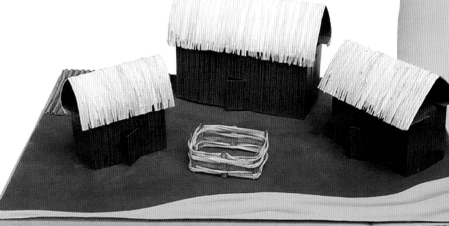

VILLAGE LIFE

Anglo-Saxon villagers all had jobs to do. The men hunted, farmed and worked in the craft houses. Women cared for young children, cooked, and spun and wove cloth. The children learnt by watching and helping their parents.

Food

Villagers kept cows, pigs, sheep, goats and chickens. They fished, hunted rabbits, and gathered fruit, nuts and berries. Wheat and barley were grown and ground-up to make bread. Meat was only eaten on special occasions. Wealthy lords and kings would hunt wild deer and boar.

Anglo-Saxon women made clothes and wove baskets, as this **reconstruction** image shows.

Cows were used to plough the fields, to grow crops like wheat and barley.

MAKE A VEGETABLE AND BARLEY STEW

All these ingredients for an Anglo-Saxon vegetable stew could be grown in the nearby fields.

Ask an adult to help you with this activity

You will need:
- 1 leek – peeled and sliced
- 1 onion – peeled and sliced
- 200 g peas
- handful of chopped cabbage
- 200 g (pearl) barley
- 1 bay leaf
- pinch of sage
- pinch of salt

1 Put all the ingredients into a saucepan. Just cover with water and bring to the boil.

2 Turn the heat down and simmer for 40 minutes or until the barley is soft.

3 Take out the bay leaf. Ladle into a soup bowl and eat with a thick slice of bread.

Modern tips
Adapt your recipe for today and add some vegetable stock and a bit of cream!

CLOTHES

People made clothes from **linen** or wool. They spun sheep's wool into **yarn** and wove it into cloth. **Dyes** from plants were used to colour the cloth blue, yellow and red. Onion skins were used to dye clothes brown.

Everyday wear

Anglo-Saxon men wore **tunics** and leggings. Women wore long dresses and head cloths. Their belts and shoes were made from leather. Children dressed like their parents. Clothes were kept in place with buckles, pins and brooches.

This beautiful belt buckle was found at Sutton Hoo (see page 18).

This reconstruction shows Anglo-Saxon women using mill stones to make flour.

MAKE A SNAKE-DESIGN BUCKLE

You will need:
- **air-drying clay**
- **ruler**
- **gold, black and green paint**

3 Leave in a safe place to dry out overnight.

1 Roll out four sausages of air-drying clay. Make them about 20 cm long and flatten one end slightly to make the snakes' heads.

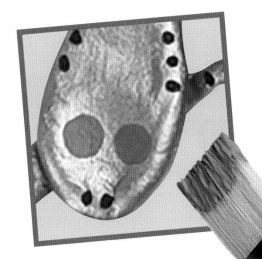

4 When your buckle is dry, decorate with gold paint and black spots. Don't forget to paint on eyes.

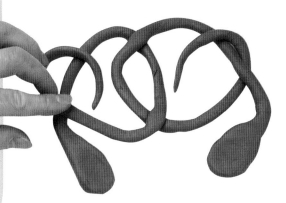

2 Arrange the four snakes in an interweaving pattern. Play around with the snakes until you are happy with your design. Then, squash the clay down where the snakes touch each other to fix in place.

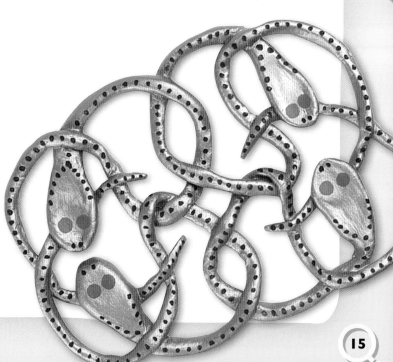

STORYTELLERS

Anglo-Saxon storytellers travelled from village to village. They sang or recited their story poems from memory. The stories were about gods, kings and battles with brave heroes who fought monsters and dragons.

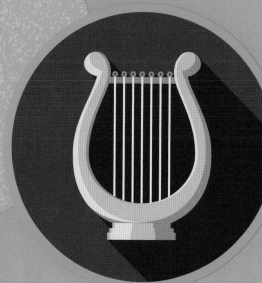

Beowulf

Storytellers played small instruments to add drama to their tales. One exciting story tells of the hero Beowulf who killed a terrible monster called Grendel. Beowulf killed many monsters during his lifetime but was eventually killed in a fight with a dragon.

Lyres, harps and pipes were small instruments that were easy to carry around.

Beowulf (centre) and companion fighting a dragon.

MAKE A LYRE

Ask an adult to help you with this activity

You will need:
- card
- pencil
- scissors
- hole punch
- glue or sticky tape
- black thread
- brown paint
- gold stickers (or foil)

bridge

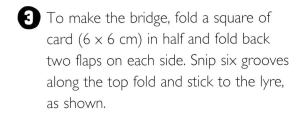

1 Copy the shape of this lyre (left) onto card, making it about as big as this page. Ask an adult to help with cutting out the centre shape.

stick bridge here

3 To make the bridge, fold a square of card (6 x 6 cm) in half and fold back two flaps on each side. Snip six grooves along the top fold and stick to the lyre, as shown.

4 Cut six lengths of black thread about 40 cm long. Thread each one through a hole at the top, over a groove in the bridge and through the bottom hole. Tie in place. Paint the lyre light brown and add gold decorations.

2 Punch six holes along the top and one hole centre bottom with a hole punch.

DEATH AND BURIAL

When the Anglo-Saxon invaders arrived in Britain, they brought their **pagan** religion with them. When they died, they were buried with things they might need in the **afterlife**.

Sutton Hoo

In 1939, an Anglo-Saxon ship burial was discovered at Sutton Hoo in Suffolk. We have learnt a lot about the man who was buried there and the **possessions** that were found with him. Both pagan and **Christian** things were buried with the Sutton Hoo man.

Things buried with the Sutton Hoo man

Weapons and armour

- An iron helmet stamped with pictures of battle scenes
- A huge shield with richly decorated fittings
- A mail-coat; an axe hammer; spears and a patterned sword

Household goods

- Silver dishes, cups and spoons
- Cooking pots
- Drinking horns

Pastimes

- A lyre
- An ivory piece for a game

Precious items

- Coins
- A gold buckle (see page 14) and clasps decorated with precious stones

The Sutton Hoo man was buried in a wooden ship 24 metres long.

Prized possessions

The Sutton Hoo man's possessions suggest he could have been a great war leader. He may have been a musician or a poet, and perhaps a generous host. Some of the items may have been gifts to show that he was well respected.

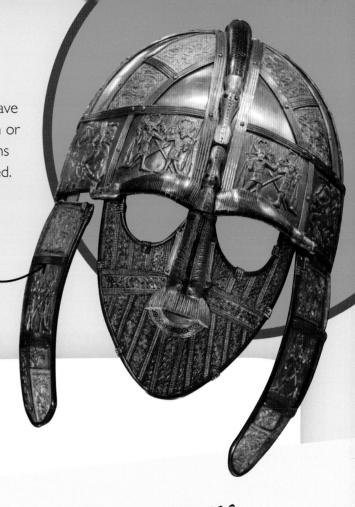

This iron helmet found at Sutton Hoo is stamped with pictures of battle scenes.

ACTIVITY

WHO WAS HE?

❶ Write a story about the Sutton Hoo man.

❷ Visit the British Museum website (www.britishmuseum.org) to search for items buried with the Sutton Hoo man.

❸ Do you think he was a king, a soldier or a farmer? Was he wealthy or poor?

❹ Draw a picture of what you think he looked like.

The Sutton Hoo man was very important. He had lots of jewels and gold

KINGS AND KINGDOMS

By 600 CE, Anglo-Saxon Britain was divided
into five main kingdoms – East Anglia,
Mercia, Northumberland, Wessex and Kent.

Offa's Dyke

Offa was a powerful king of Mercia. In 787 CE, he
built a great ditch to protect his kingdom. It was
270 kilometres long. It is known as Offa's Dyke and
you can still see it today running along the border
between Wales and England.

This map shows the five main
kingdoms of Anglo-Saxon Britain.

Alfred the Great

In 871 CE, Alfred became king of Wessex. He is known as
Alfred the Great. He fought against **Viking** invaders from
Scandinavia and drove them out of his kingdom. The Vikings
settled in the north-east of what is now England.

King Alfred defended the kingdom
of Wessex from Viking invaders.

Famous faces

The Anglo-Saxons used silver pennies for everyday buying and selling. They had the king's head on one side, and details of where, when and who made the coin on the other.

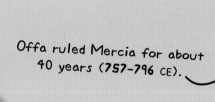

Offa ruled Mercia for about 40 years (757–796 CE).

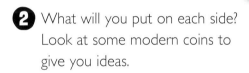

ACTIVITY

DESIGN A COIN

Design your own coin, pretending you were a rich king like Alfred or Offa.

You will need:
- **thick card**
- **pencil**
- **scissors**
- **metallic paint**
- **felt-tip pens**

1 Draw two circles on thick card bigger than a coin to give you room for your design.

2 What will you put on each side? Look at some modern coins to give you ideas.

3 Cut out and decorate your coin with metallic paint and felt-tip pens.

4 What does your coin say about you?

GODS AND GODDESSES

The Anglo-Saxons believed in many gods and goddesses. Four of the most famous are Tiw, Woden, Frigg and Thor.

Pagan festivals

Some of the Christian **festivals** we celebrate today took the place of pagan festivals. **Easter**, for example, was the festival of Eostre, the goddess of Spring.

Eostre was known as the goddess of rebirth and 'new beginnings'.

Tiw was the god of war and justice among the gods.

Woden was the god of wisdom. He rode an eight-legged horse with wings.

Frigg, goddess of marriage, was Woden's wife.

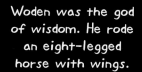

Thor, god of thunder, had a hammer that came back to him after he threw it.

Harvest time

Our **harvest** festival was the festival of Nerthus, the earth mother. A corn dolly was the symbol of Nerthus. Corn dollies, made from straw, were made to bring good luck in the next year.

Corn dollies were used to give thanks for the harvest and for the hope of good times ahead.

MAKE A 'STRAW' CORN DOLLY

You will need:

- **9 art straws**
- **yellow paint**
- **ribbon**

1 Make three groups of three art straws.

2 Plait each group half way and paint yellow.

3 When dry, tie the ends of each plait with a red ribbon. Tie the loose ends together at the top of the plaits. Then tie with ribbon again at the very top.

RELIGION

In 597 CE, the head of the Christian church Pope Gregory sent **missionaries** to Britain to convert the Anglo-Saxons to Christianity. A hundred years later, every British king was Christian.

Pope Gregory wanted to spread Christianity among the pagan Anglo-Saxons.

Monasteries

Churches and **monasteries** were built all over Britain. Monasteries were places of worship and learning where **monks** copied and illustrated books by hand and taught boys to read and write.

The ruins of the monastery on the island of Lindisfarne.

Important texts

One famous monk was Saint Bede (673–735 CE). He wrote many important things in **Latin** including a chronicle of English history from the time of the Roman invasion. The Lindisfarne **Gospels** are thought to have been written and illustrated in 710–721 CE by just one monk, Eadfrith the Bishop of Lindisfarne.

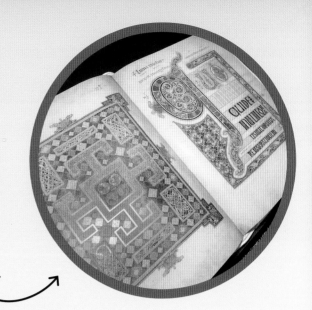

The Lindisfarne Gospels are beautifully illustrated. They recount the life of Christ.

ACTIVITY

DECORATED LETTERS

Letters at the beginning of a page in the Lindisfarne Gospels were often decorated with pictures that illustrated the writing.

You will need:
- **paper**
- **pencil and felt-tip pens**
- **gold and silver pens**

1 Design and colour the letters of your initials.

2 What pictures could tell us something about you? Use gold and silver pens as well as bright colours.

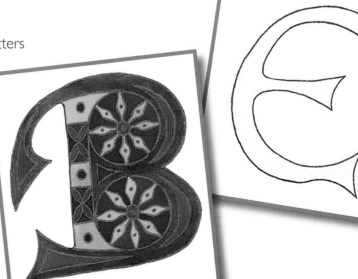

RUNES AND WRITING

Anglo-Saxon was originally written in letters called runes, which were thought to have magic meanings. Runes were made up of straight lines. This made runes easier for people to carve.

Changing times

The word 'rune' means secret or mystery. The Anglo-Saxons thought some runes could be used for spells or charms. When the Anglo-Saxons turned to Christianity, however, more people began to use the Roman alphabet and runes gradually died away. The Anglo-Saxon Chronicle (see page 7), for example, was written in Anglo-Saxon, but using the Roman alphabet we use in English today.

Carved runes can be seen on this whalebone casket.

Some runes were thought to be magical or to bring good luck.

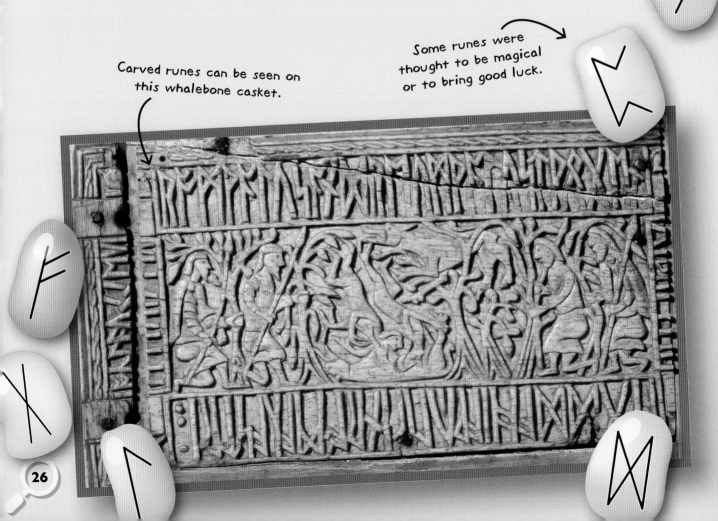

CARVE AN ANGLO-SAXON PATTERN

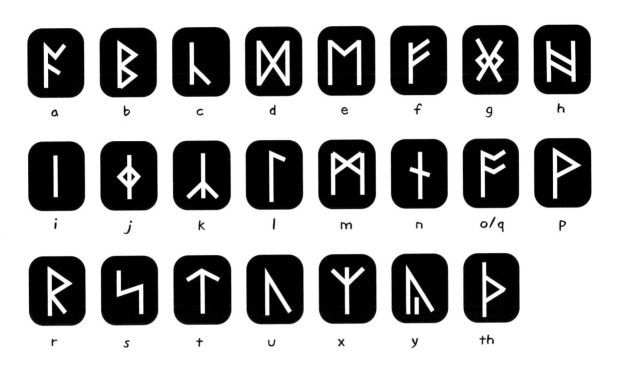

a	b	c	d	e	f	g	h
i	j	k	l	m	n	o/q	p
r	s	t	u	x	y	th	

You will need:
- **air-drying clay**
- **modelling knife**
- **paper and pencil**

1 Roll out a piece of air-drying clay until it is roughly 8 mm thick. Cut out a square about 15 cm × 15 cm with a modelling knife.

2 Carve an Anglo-Saxon pattern onto the tile. Look in books or on the Internet for ideas.

3 Decide what you want to write underneath it – your name, a place, a mysterious word. Work it out in runes on a piece of paper first.

Glossary

afterlife

Anglo-Saxons believed in the afterlife – life after death. They were buried with things they would need in the afterlife.

Christianity

Christianity is a religion based on the belief in one God and the teachings of Jesus Christ.

dye

A dye is a substance used to colour materials.

Easter

Easter is the English name for the Christian spring festival to celebrate Jesus rising from the dead.

festival

A festival is a celebration, such as a feast or a party, held on a special religious occasion.

Gospels

The Gospels are the first four books of the New Testament, part of the Christian Bible, telling of the life of Christ.

harvest

A harvest is the gathering of crops when they are ripe. A harvest festival is held in the Autumn.

invade

To invade is to enter another country by force, with the intention of taking it over.

Latin

Latin is the language spoken and written by the Ancient Romans.

linen

Linen is a strong cloth made from the fibres of the flax plant.

lyre

A lyre is a small stringed instrument, similar to a harp.

missionary

A missionary is a person sent to another country to persuade the people living there to change their religious beliefs.

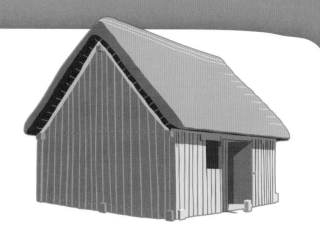

monastery

A monastery is a place where monks live and worship.

monk

A monk is a member of a religious community who lives and works in a monastery.

pagan

Pagan is a term used to describe religions where its followers worship many gods.

possessions

Possessions are things that somebody owns or has with them.

reconstruction

A reconstruction is a model of how something would have been in the past.

settlement

A settlement is a new place where people have decided to live.

thatched

A thatched roof is a roof made from straw or reeds.

tribe

A tribe is a group of people who live together and who have the same background, religion and leader.

tunic

A tunic was a long top worn by an Anglo-Saxon man.

Vikings

The Vikings were pirates and traders who came from Scandinavia.

warriors

Warriors are soldiers who fight in battle.

yarn

Yarn is wool twisted into a long thread that can be used for knitting and weaving.

Quiz

1 **When did the Anglo-Saxons invade Britain?**

a) 3rd and 4th centuries
b) 5th and 6th centuries
c) 7th and 8th centuries
d) 9th and 10th centuries

2 **Where did the Anglo-Saxons land in Britain?**

a) east and south coasts
b) north and west coasts
c) north and south coasts
d) south and west coasts

3 **'Ham' was the Anglo-Saxon word for:**

a) pig
b) hill
c) hedge
d) settlement

4 **Where was an Anglo-Saxon ship burial discovered in 1939?**

a) Sutton Coldfield
b) Sutton Hoo
c) Sutton Place
d) Long Sutton

5 **Name the famous monster killed by Beowulf:**

a) Greta
b) Grace
c) Grendel
d) Griselda

6 **Which of the following was NOT a main kingdom of Anglo-Saxon Britain?**

a) East Anglia
b) Mercia
c) Wessex
d) Wales

7 **Which pagan goddess is associated with a harvest festival?**

a) Harvey
b) Harvest
c) Nerthus
d) Nereida

8 **Can you match the weekday to the name of an Anglo-Saxon god or goddess?**

a) Tuesday   i) Thor
b) Wednesday   ii) Frigg
c) Thursday   iii) Tiw
d) Friday   iv) Woden

9 Which Pope helped to bring Christianity to Anglo-Saxon Britain?

a) Paul
b) Peter
c) John
d) Gregory

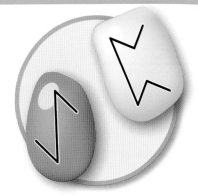

10 Runes were written in straight lines. Why was this useful?

a) they were easier to see
b) they were easier to carve
c) they were easier to copy
d) the Anglo-Saxons didn't like circles

ANSWERS 1b, 2a, 3d, 4b, 5c, 6d, 7c, 8 aiii, biv, ci, dii, 9d, 10b

FURTHER INFORMATION

BOOKS

Explore! Anglo-Saxons by Jane Bingham, Wayland

The Genius of: The Anglo-Saxons by Izzi Howell, Franklin Watts

Found! Anglo-Saxon Britain by Moira Butterfield, Franklin Watts

Invaders and Raiders: The Anglo-Saxons Are Coming! by Paul Mason, Franklin Watts

WEBSITES

Discover fun facts about the Anglo-Saxons www.natgeokids.com/uk/discover/history/general-history/anglo-saxons

Learn more about life in Anglo-Saxon times www.bbc.co.uk/bitesize/topics/zxsbcdm

Find out more about the Anglo-Saxons, their lifestyle and beliefs www.dkfindout.com/uk/history/anglo-saxons

Watch a video about the reign of Alfred the Great www.bbc.co.uk/teach/school-radio/history-ks2-anglo-saxons-alfred-the-great/zmwbbdm

Index

Titles in the DISCOVER AND DO! HISTORY series

- Invasion
- Warriors
- Settlers
- Village life
- Clothes
- Storytellers
- Death and burial
- Kings and kingdoms
- Gods and goddesses
- Religion
- Runes and writing

- The Egyptians
- The River Nile
- Egyptian life
- Clothes
- Hair and make-up
- Writing
- Gods and goddesses
- The Pharaoh
- Temple life
- The pyramids
- The afterlife

- The Greeks
- City states
- Daily life
- Childhood
- Clothes
- Religion and myths
- Olympic games
- Writing
- Theatre
- Learning
- Famous Greeks

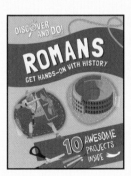

- The Romans
- Roman emperors
- The army
- Life in Roman times
- Houses
- Childhood
- Letters and numbers
- Entertainment
- Roman baths
- Roman towns
- Gods and myths

- The Tudors
- Henry VIII
- Life at court
- Tudor homes
- Tudor London
- Street life
- Elizabeth I
- Exploration
- Tudor childhood
- Food
- Theatre

- The Vikings
- Sea journeys
- Warriors
- Viking raids
- Viking houses
- Daily life
- Viking crafts
- Pastimes
- Life and death
- Gods and legends
- Famous Vikings

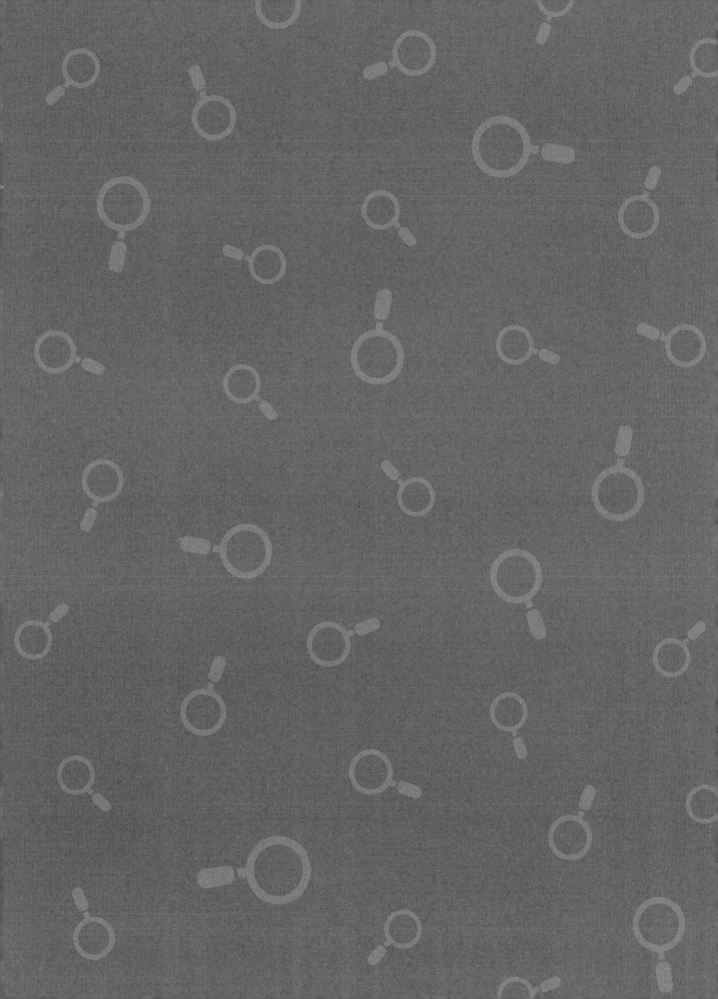